DINOSAUR WARS

WRITTEN BY DR PHIL MANNING

ILLUSTRATED BY PETER MINISTER

Ticktock

An Hachette UK Company
www.hachette.co.uk

First published in Great Britain in 2014 by Ticktock,
an imprint of Octopus Publishing Group Ltd
Endeavour House
189 Shaftesbury Avenue
London
WC2H 8JY
www.octopusbooks.co.uk
www.ticktockbooks.co.uk

ISBN 978 1 78325 0 424

A CIP record for this book is available from the British Library.

Printed and bound in China
1 3 5 7 9 10 8 6 4 2

Project Editor: Carey Scott
Design: Perfect Bound Ltd and Claire Yeo
Publisher: Samantha Sweeney
Managing Editor: Karen Rigden
Senior Production Manager: Peter Hunt

Picture Credits
Dr Phil Manning: 32, 76, 77; **Fotolia** Aldaer 46. 48; Galyna Andrushko 30, 66; Jörg Hackemann 70; Juan Cristóbal
Garcí 60. 62; Kelly Marken 38; Les Cunliffe 56; Mariusz Blach 42; Sinelyov 34; Vvoe 18 **Shutterstock** Galyna
Andrushko 14; Jill Battaglia 52; Mikhail Kolesnikov 6; Rudi Venter 22; Spirit of America 26; Ysbrand Cosijn 10
Thinkstock demarfa 25; Joe Pogliano 50 **United States Geological Survey** 4 centre

CONTENTS

The Age of the Dinosaurs · 4

DAWN OF THE DINOSAURS

Jaws! · 6
Eoraptor vs Herrerasaurus · 8
Fresh Meat · 10
Dilophosaurus vs Anchisaurus · 12
Cornered · 14
Megalosaurus vs Camptosaurus · 16

DANGEROUS DINOSAURS

Predator Trap · 18
Allosaurus vs Stegosaurus · 20
Clashing Cousins · 22
Archaeopteryx vs Compsognathus · 24
Claws on Armour · 26
Utahraptor vs Gastonia · 28

THE HUNTERS AND THE HUNTED

Surprise Attack · 30
Iguanodon vs Neovenator · 32
The Earth Shakes · 34
Sauroposeidon vs Acrocanthosaurus · 36
Cretaceous Kill · 38
Tenontosaurus vs Deinonychus · 40
Crocodile Jaws · 42
Kaprosuchus vs Carcharodontosaurus · 44

PACK-HUNTERS AND PRICKLY PREY

Under Cover · 46
The Fight Back · 48
Velociraptor vs Protoceratops · 50
Wounding Teeth · 52
Troodon vs Avaceratops · 54
The Last Lunge · 56
Gorgosaurus vs Parasaurolophus · 58

BATTLE OF THE TITANS

A Chance Ambush · 60
In For The Kill · 62
Albertosaurus vs Hypacrosaurus · 64
Desert Encounter · 66
Tarbosaurus vs Tarchia · 68
Killing Blow · 70
Tyrannosaurus rex vs Triceratops · 72

The Results! · 74
Real-life Battles · 76
Glossary · 78
Index · 80

TRIASSIC		EARLY JURASSIC		LATE JURASSIC
230 mya	220 mya	210 mya	200 mya	190 mya

180 mya   170 mya   160 mya   150 m

THE AGE OF THE DINOSAURS

For 165 million years, the world was ruled by the dinosaurs. Around 900 different species have been identified. Some were gentle and docile plant-eaters and others were fearsome predators. They could be as small as a chicken or as big as a bus!

What's the Time Mr Dinosaur?

As you read this book check out this timeline at the top of the facts and stats pages. The featured dinosaurs will be bright, so you'll be able to see in which period they lived, and how many millions of years ago (mya) that was.

The world was a very different place when dinosaurs roamed the Earth, fossils of the same creatures have been found in different continents, which shows that at some point those continents were joined together in a single landmass, called Pangaea. It began to break up in the Middle Jurassic Period.

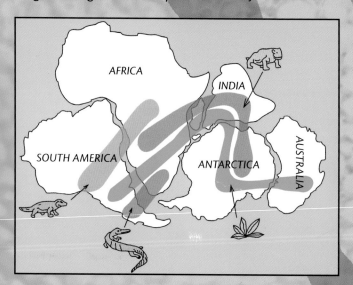

The Mesozoic Era

Dinosaurs lived during the Mesozoic Era, which scientists divide into three time periods. The earliest is called the **Triassic Period**, 251–200 million years ago (mya). This is when the first dinosaurs evolved. The **Jurassic Period**, 200–145 mya, was the height of the dinosaurs' reign, when the most massive species roamed the world. In the **Cretaceous Period**, 145–66 mya, tyrannosaurs and horned dinosaurs appeared.

Dinosaur Relations

All dinosaurs belong to one of two orders – the lizard-hipped saurischians and the bird-hipped ornithischians. The horned and armoured dinosaurs are in the plant-eating (herbivore) ornithischian order. The saurischian order included both herbivores and meat-eaters (carnivores).

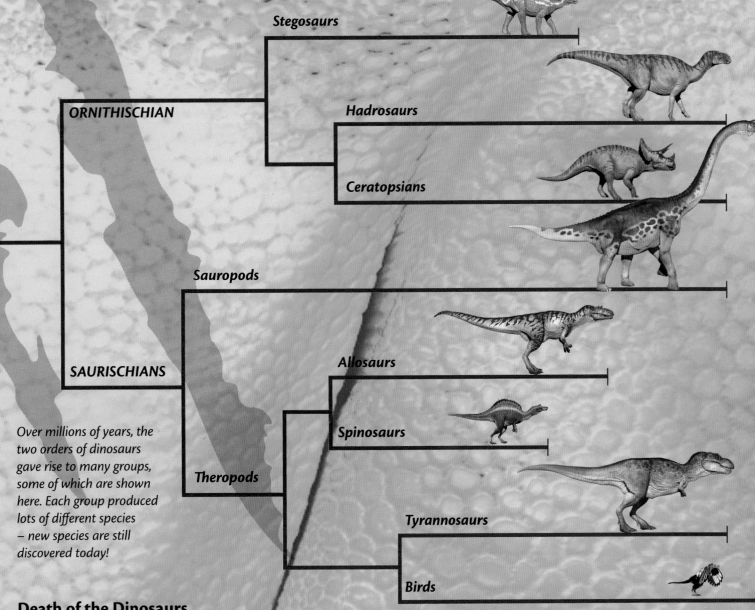

Stegosaurs

ORNITHISCHIAN

Hadrosaurs

Ceratopsians

Sauropods

SAURISCHIANS

Allosaurs

Over millions of years, the two orders of dinosaurs gave rise to many groups, some of which are shown here. Each group produced lots of different species – new species are still discovered today!

Spinosaurs

Theropods

Tyrannosaurs

Birds

Death of the Dinosaurs

The reign of the dinosaurs ended suddenly 66 million years ago. The combination of a giant comet crashing into Earth, vast volcanic eruptions and climate change caused the deaths of around 75 per cent of all animals on the planet. Bird descendants of the theropod dinosaurs survived the mass extinction.

Jaws!

We are in the Triassic Period. The first dinosaurs have evolved from their reptilian ancestors. They are agile, fast, clawed and sharp-toothed carnivores. In what is now South America, two dinosaur species, *Herrerasaurus* and *Eoraptor*, compete for food. *Herrerasaurus* is a big beast, weighing about as much as a polar bear, but *Eoraptor* is the faster animal. *Herrerasaurus* gives chase to three *Eoraptors*, who have dared to enter its cave in search of a possible carcass to steal. One is already wounded, and all three are retreating as fast as they can but the snapping jaws are drawing in.

HERRERASAURUS

How to say it: *Huh-rer-ra-saw-rus*

BATTLE FEATURES

KILLER ABILITY	5
SPEED AND POWER	6
BRUTE STRENGTH	3
BODY MASS	4
BRAIN POWER	6
TOTAL	**24**

Herrerasaurus means **Herrera's lizard**, after the Argentinian rancher who found the first fossil specimen. When a **complete skeleton** was discovered, it showed that *Herrerasaurus* was a **predatory dinosaur**. Amazingly, humans are much closer in time to *Tyrannosaurus rex* than *Herrerasaurus* was, but experts believe that this early predator was in fact **T. *rex*'s distant ancestor.**

1.5 m

1 m

CREATURE FEATURE

Leaf-shaped teeth in the very front of its jaws.

0.5 m

350 kg

0 m

Short arms ending in long hands.

The biggest dinosaur predator of its time.

4 m   3 m   1 m   0 m

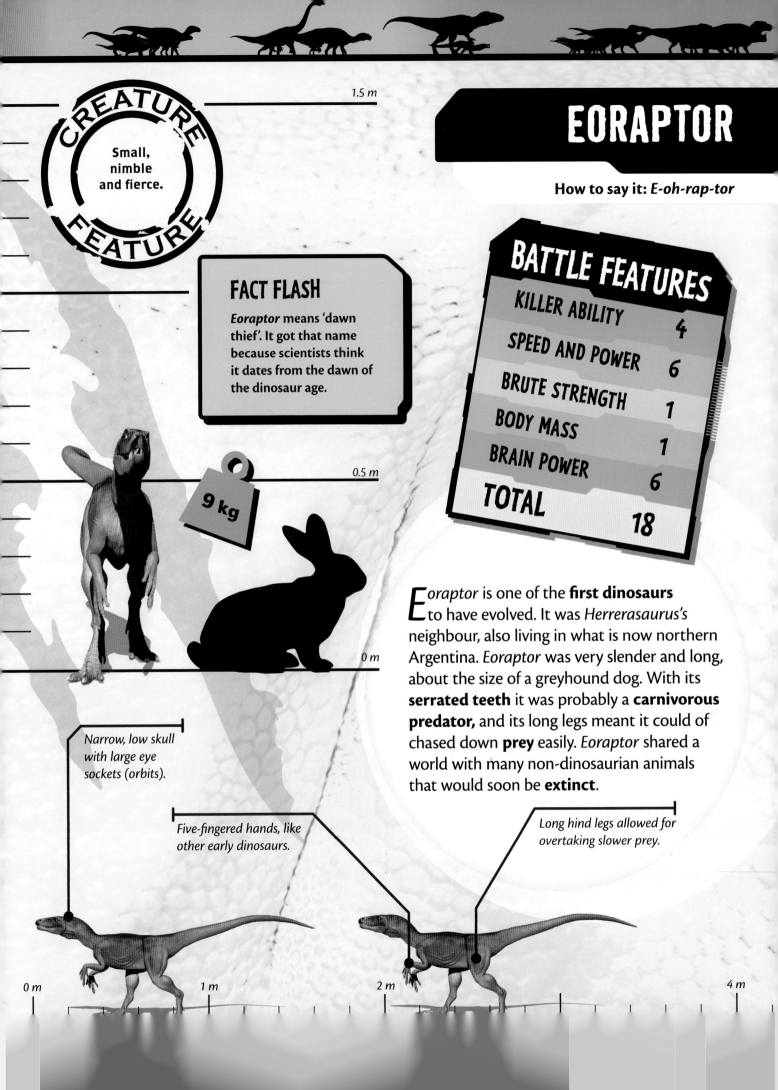

CREATURE FEATURE

Small, nimble and fierce.

EORAPTOR

How to say it: E-oh-rap-tor

FACT FLASH

Eoraptor means 'dawn thief'. It got that name because scientists think it dates from the dawn of the dinosaur age.

9 kg

BATTLE FEATURES

KILLER ABILITY	4
SPEED AND POWER	6
BRUTE STRENGTH	1
BODY MASS	1
BRAIN POWER	6
TOTAL	18

Eoraptor is one of the **first dinosaurs** to have evolved. It was *Herrerasaurus's* neighbour, also living in what is now northern Argentina. *Eoraptor* was very slender and long, about the size of a greyhound dog. With its **serrated teeth** it was probably a **carnivorous predator,** and its long legs meant it could of chased down **prey** easily. *Eoraptor* shared a world with many non-dinosaurian animals that would soon be **extinct.**

Narrow, low skull with large eye sockets (orbits).

Five-fingered hands, like other early dinosaurs.

Long hind legs allowed for overtaking slower prey.

1.5 m

0.5 m

0 m

0 m   1 m   2 m   4 m

Fresh Meat

The Jurassic Period has begun. The dinosaurs are getting bigger and becoming more dominant. Plant-eating dinosaurs, such as *Anchisaurus*, have now evolved. These docile animals are only about the weight of a small human and can become prey for their bigger carnivorous cousins. One such carnivore, *Dilophosaurus*, gives chase to a family of *Anchisaurus*. The herbivores scuttle away, seeking refuge in the safety of their herd. Will *Dilophosaurus* manage to pick one of them off?

DILOPHOSAURUS

How to say it: *Die-low-four-saw-rus*

193 mya

2 m

350 kg

Strange crests on head, probably for attracting a mate.

BATTLE FEATURES

KILLER ABILITY	5
SPEED AND POWER	5
BRUTE STRENGTH	4
BODY MASS	4
BRAIN POWER	3
TOTAL	**21**

CREST CREATIVITY

Lots of dinosaurs had fancy crests on their heads, but scientists aren't always sure why. They may have been for intimidating predators and/or attracting mates.

They could have been used for fighting, but often they don't seem sturdy enough. Perhaps it just made it easier to identify members or males and females of a group's own species!

*D*ilophosaurus gets its name from the impressive roof to its skull – it means **two-crested lizard**. *Dilophosaurus*'s crests were too delicate to use for fighting so they were probably just decorative. **Fossil remains** of this carnivore have been found in the USA and in India, showing that it lived in a very large area but not in different landmasses – during the **Early Jurassic Period** all the continents were still joined together.

Notch in upper jaw may indicate a fish-eater.

Computer simulations calculate a top running speed of 37 k/ph (23 mph).

Big nostrils suggests an excellent sense of smell.

7 m   6 m   5 m   4 m   3 m   2 m   1 m   0 m

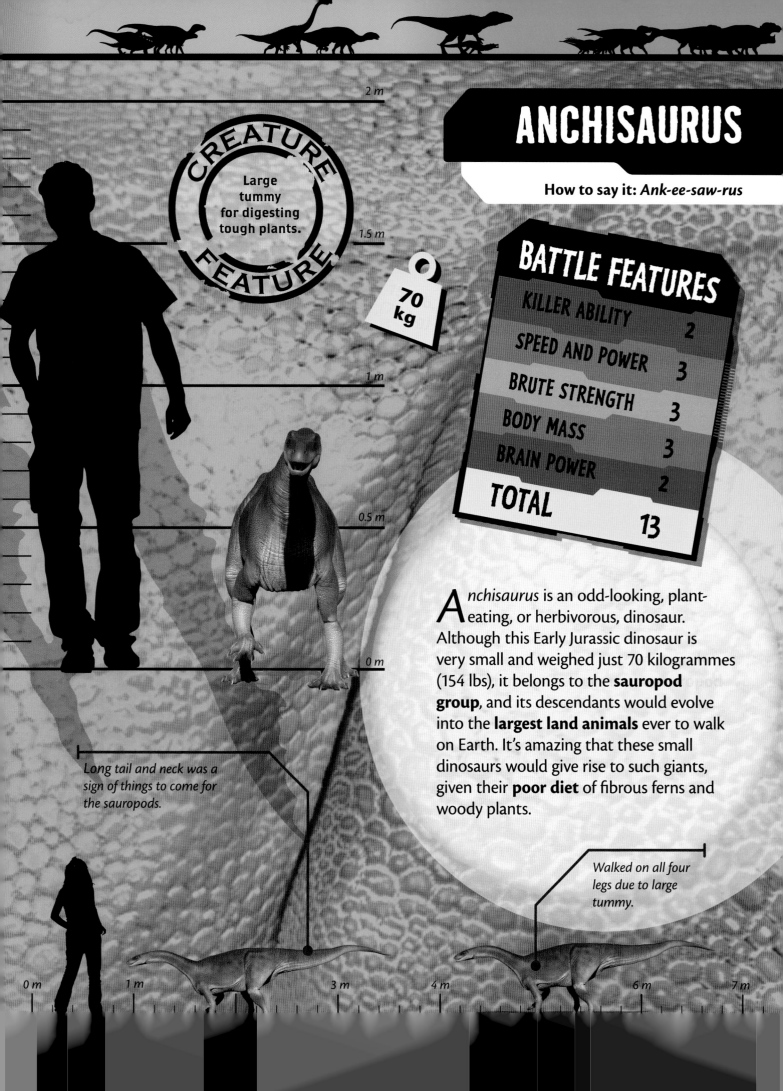

ANCHISAURUS

How to say it: *Ank-ee-saw-rus*

CREATURE FEATURE

Large tummy for digesting tough plants.

70 kg

BATTLE FEATURES

KILLER ABILITY	2
SPEED AND POWER	3
BRUTE STRENGTH	3
BODY MASS	3
BRAIN POWER	2
TOTAL	**13**

Anchisaurus is an odd-looking, plant-eating, or herbivorous, dinosaur. Although this Early Jurassic dinosaur is very small and weighed just 70 kilogrammes (154 lbs), it belongs to the **sauropod group**, and its descendants would evolve into the **largest land animals** ever to walk on Earth. It's amazing that these small dinosaurs would give rise to such giants, given their **poor diet** of fibrous ferns and woody plants.

Long tail and neck was a sign of things to come for the sauropods.

Walked on all four legs due to large tummy.

2 m

1.5 m

1 m

0.5 m

0 m

0 m 1 m 3 m 4 m 6 m 7 m

Cornered

The young predator *Megalosaurus* and an adult *Camptosaurus* are evenly matched in body mass. They circle one another, each trying to gain an advantage. Suddenly, the predator makes its move. It opens its huge jaws, and starts to back the prey toward a wall of boulders. Cornered, *Camptosaurus* turns to face its enemy. Will the young *Megalosaurus's* lack of hunting experience provide the lucky break its victim needs, or will this encounter be fatal?

4 m

MEGALOSAURUS

How to say it: *Meg-A-low-saw-rus*

BATTLE FEATURES

KILLER ABILITY	6
SPEED AND POWER	6
BRUTE STRENGTH	5
BODY MASS	6
BRAIN POWER	3
TOTAL	**26**

CREATURE FEATURE Unknown, as fragmentary skeleton allows experts to only estimate body size and mass.

2 m

1000 kg

In 1824, British scientist William Buckland named the fossilized bones of a **giant, lizard-type animal**. He called it *Megalosaurus*, which means **great lizard**. It would be another 20 years before the word **dinosaur** was coined. **No complete skeleton** has been discovered yet, so scientists can't say exactly how *Megalosaurus* looked, but they do know that it was carnivorous and belonged to the theropod group.

0 m

Serrated teeth grew up to 10 cm (4 in) long.

Heavy limb bones for a theropod.

Hands with three-fingers.

9 m   8 m   7 m   6 m   4 m   2 m   1 m   0 m

CAMPTOSAURUS

How to say it: *Camp-toe-saw-rus*

FACT FLASH

Dinosaurs like *Camptosaurus* had a beak instead of soft lips, to help with chopping up its leafy food.

CREATURE FEATURE

Was probably both bipedal and quadrupedal – could walk on hind legs and on all fours.

900 kg

BATTLE FEATURES

KILLER ABILITY	2
SPEED AND POWER	4
BRUTE STRENGTH	3
BODY MASS	4
BRAIN POWER	3
TOTAL	16

Camptosaurus is a Jurassic dinosaur whose fossil remains have been found in both **North America and Europe**. This herbivore gets its name from its long, **supple backbone**, *Camptosaurus* meaning **flexible lizard**. Its three-toed feet give the name to the **ornithopod** 'bird-feet' dinosaurs, a group in the ornithischian order. The **tightly packed teeth** in its cheek, combined with its beak were perfect for cutting and processing the tough Jurassic vegetation.

Five-fingered hands, the first three with hoof-like tips.

Deep, sturdy tail supported by long, powerful muscles.

1 m

0 m

0 m   1 m   2 m   4 m   5 m   6 m   7 m   8 m   9 m

Predator Trap

The rainy season is long overdue and predators are stalking the last few water holes. *Stegosaurus* approaches a rapidly drying lakebed and laps thirstily. It pauses and glances over its shoulder – pushing its head directly into the waiting jaws of *Allosaurus*! Will the bones of this herbivore soon join those of other prey that litter the water holes? Or will it fight back with its powerful tail and killer spikes?

ALLOSAURUS

How to say it: *Al-oh-saw-rus*

5 m

BATTLE FEATURES

KILLER ABILITY	8
SPEED AND POWER	7
BRUTE STRENGTH	8
BODY MASS	7
BRAIN POWER	6
TOTAL	**36**

CREATURE FEATURE

Enlarged piece of bone above each eye socket, for display or for reinforcing the bite.

2000 kg

By the Late Jurassic Period, the world of the dinosaurs was changing. **Giant, predatory dinosaurs** were now roaming the world. One of them was *Allosaurus*. This **theropod** was heavier than an elephant, with a **massive jaw,** strong arms and powerful, muscular legs. *Allosaurus* preyed on the plant-eating dinosaurs and may have hunted by **ambushing** its victims.

2 m

0 m

Many of its bones were hollow, just like modern birds' bones.

Three large fingers tipped with sharp claws.

12 m 11 m 10 m 9 m 8 m 7 m 6 m 5 m 4 m 3 m 2 m 1 m 0 m

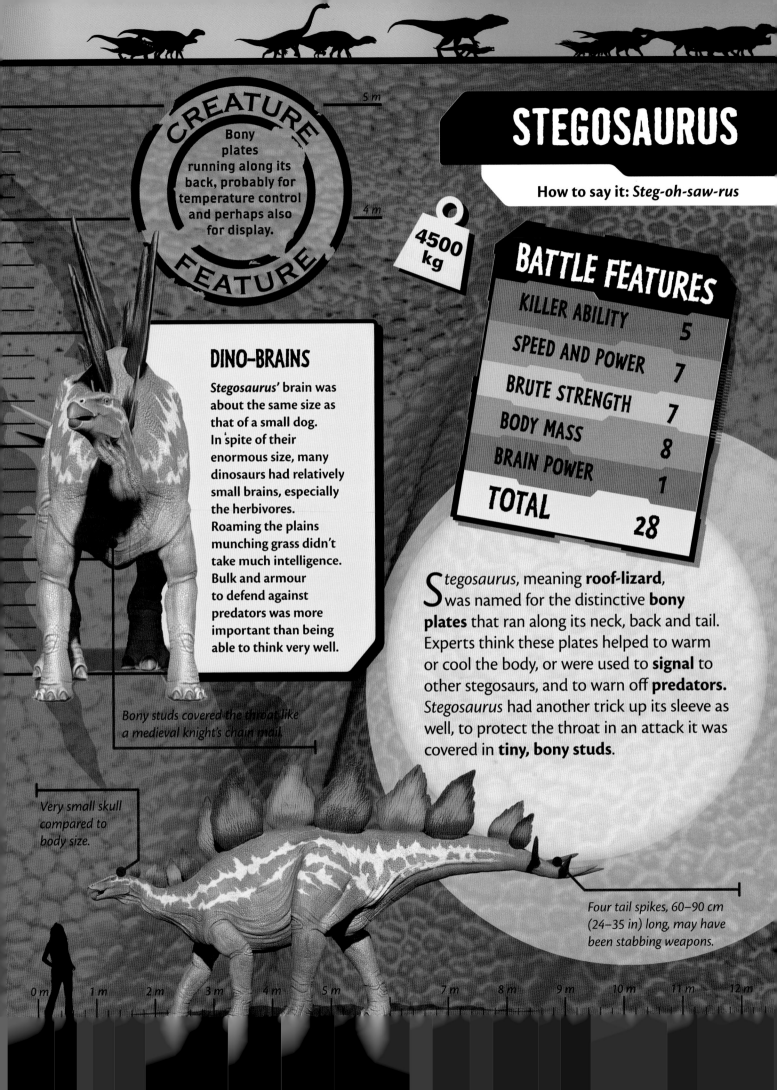

Bony plates running along its back, probably for temperature control and perhaps also for display.

STEGOSAURUS

How to say it: *Steg-oh-saw-rus*

4500 kg

BATTLE FEATURES

KILLER ABILITY	5
SPEED AND POWER	7
BRUTE STRENGTH	7
BODY MASS	8
BRAIN POWER	1
TOTAL	28

DINO-BRAINS

Stegosaurus' brain was about the same size as that of a small dog. In spite of their enormous size, many dinosaurs had relatively small brains, especially the herbivores. Roaming the plains munching grass didn't take much intelligence. Bulk and armour to defend against predators was more important than being able to think very well.

Stegosaurus, meaning **roof-lizard**, was named for the distinctive **bony plates** that ran along its neck, back and tail. Experts think these plates helped to warm or cool the body, or were used to **signal** to other stegosaurs, and to warn off **predators.** *Stegosaurus* had another trick up its sleeve as well, to protect the throat in an attack it was covered in **tiny, bony studs**.

Bony studs covered the throat like a medieval knight's chain mail.

Very small skull compared to body size.

Four tail spikes, 60–90 cm (24–35 in) long, may have been stabbing weapons.

0 m 1 m 2 m 3 m 4 m 5 m 7 m 8 m 9 m 10 m 11 m 12 m

Clashing Cousins

The late Jurassic Period, has given rise to a wide variety of dinosaurs, some have even evolved into flying, bird-like animals. Here an *Archaeopteryx*, 'the first bird', leaps into the air, kicking its sharp talons at *Compsognathus*. Its enemy is its closest relative – like two sides to the same coin. The *Archaeopteryx* was just looking for a break from searching for fish and stumbled into wrong territory – now it faces a standoff with the fierce *Compsognathus*. Who will back down? Who is the superior fighter, the 'first bird' or its land-living cousin?

ARCHAEOPTERYX

How to say it: *Arc-ee-op-tricks*

BATTLE FEATURES

KILLER ABILITY	4
SPEED AND POWER	4
BRUTE STRENGTH	1
BODY MASS	1
BRAIN POWER	4
TOTAL	14

EARLY BIRD

This amazing fossil was discovered in Germany in 1861. You can make out some of its distinctive bird and dinosaur features of feathers, teeth, claws and the bony tail!

CREATURE FEATURE

Cross between a theropod dinosaur and a modern bird.

Sharp, curved claws adapted to help climb or perch.

60 cm

This small, feathered dinosaur is known as the first bird, but *Archaeopteryx* had features of both a bird and a dinosaur! It had the **long bony tail and toothed jaws** of its theropod ancestors but the **wishbone and wings** of modern birds. *Archaeopteryx* could almost certainly fly, and would have hunted its prey along the shores of the shallow seas and lagoons of Late Jurassic Europe.

0.5 kg

0 m

Fused collar bones form the u-shaped wishbone of all birds.

Head and neck were probably unfeathered.

Tips of flight feathers were likely to have been black.

1.5 m

1 m

0.5 m

0 m

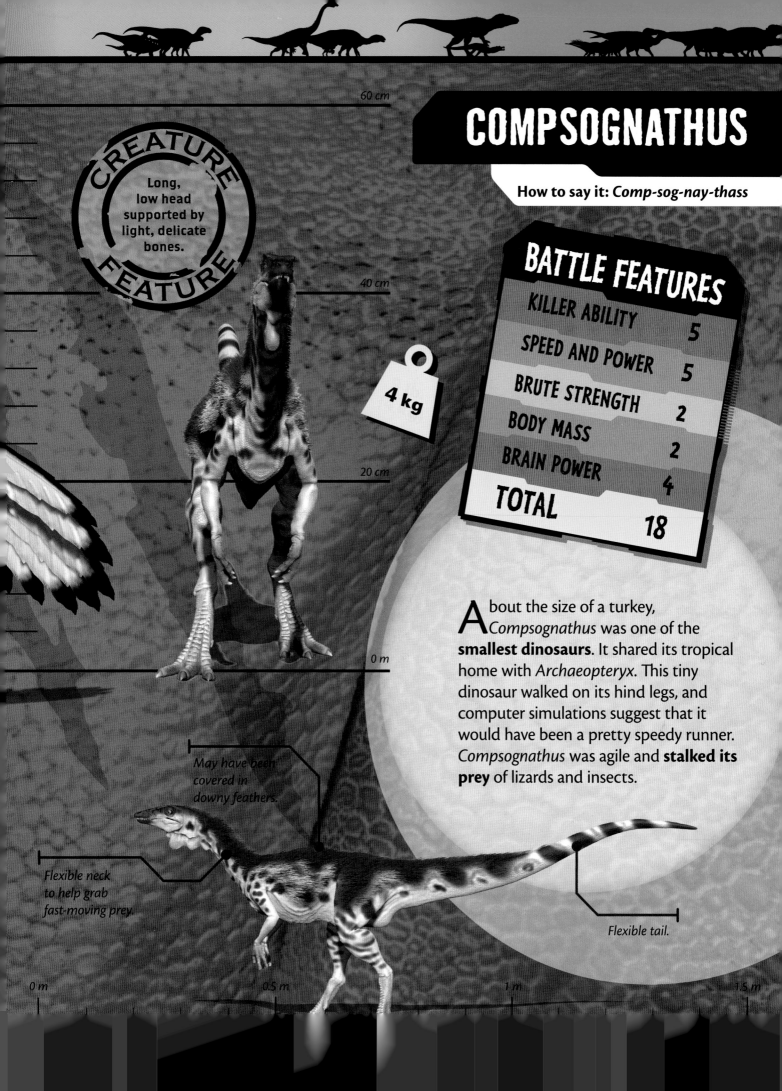

60 cm

CREATURE FEATURE

Long, low head supported by light, delicate bones.

40 cm

4 kg

20 cm

0 m

COMPSOGNATHUS

How to say it: *Comp-sog-nay-thass*

BATTLE FEATURES

KILLER ABILITY	5
SPEED AND POWER	5
BRUTE STRENGTH	2
BODY MASS	2
BRAIN POWER	4
TOTAL	**18**

About the size of a turkey, *Compsognathus* was one of the **smallest dinosaurs**. It shared its tropical home with *Archaeopteryx*. This tiny dinosaur walked on its hind legs, and computer simulations suggest that it would have been a pretty speedy runner. *Compsognathus* was agile and **stalked its prey** of lizards and insects.

May have been covered in downy feathers.

Flexible neck to help grab fast-moving prey.

Flexible tail.

0 m   0.5 m   1 m   1.5 m

Claws on Armour

The huge, sickle-shaped claws of *Utahraptor* have found a grip between the bony spikes of its dumpy *Gastonia* prey. It has not eaten for over a week and will now tackle anything – even this tank of a beast. The stricken *Gastonia* spins around, trying to unbalance its piggy-back attacker. But *Utahraptor* hangs on, biting again and again into the few unarmoured areas of the ankylosaur's back with its razor-sharp teeth. If it can just keep this up, the battle could soon be over. Can *Utahraptor* really fell a prey such as *Gastonia*?

UTAHRAPTOR

How to say it: *Utah-rap-tor*

BATTLE FEATURES

KILLER ABILITY	8
SPEED AND POWER	8
BRUTE STRENGTH	3
BODY MASS	3
BRAIN POWER	8
TOTAL	**30**

TERRIBLE CLAW

Utahraptor probably used its dreadful claw to grab hold of its prey. Then *Utahraptor* would sink its sharp teeth into the flesh.

3 m

500 kg

CREATURE FEATURE

Massive curved claw on second toe, probably for climbing and holding onto prey.

This sickle-clawed dinosaur was named after the US state in which it was discovered – its name means **Utah's predator**. It was the largest member of the **dromaeosauridae** group – **bird-like**, bipedal dinosaurs of the Cretaceous Period. The claw on its second toe was enlarged into a big, hook-like weapon. *Utahraptor* was an intelligent dinosaur and may have been **top predator** of its home area.

0 m

Toe claw up to 38 cm (15 in) long.

Stiff tail typical of dromaeosaur dinosaurs.

Long, muscular hind legs for speed and strength.

Jaws housed long, narrow teeth.

7 m   6 m   5 m   4 m   2 m   1 m   0 m

3 m

2 m

CREATURE FEATURE

Wide, flat, bony spines covering the neck, back and tail.

1500 kg

GASTONIA

How to say it: *Gas-toe-near*

BATTLE FEATURES

KILLER ABILITY	3
SPEED AND POWER	5
BRUTE STRENGTH	6
BODY MASS	6
BRAIN POWER	3
TOTAL	23

*G*astonia was an **ankylosaur** of the Cretaceous Period. These herbivorous dinosaurs were built for protection against carnivorous predators. **Rows of bony spines** running from *Gastonia's* head to its tail provided a **living suit of armour**. In an attack, *Gastonia's* short limbs meant it could quickly lie down and display its **spiky armour**. *Gastonia's* tough beak was designed to harvest its food, and its small, **leaf-shaped, serrated teeth** were adapted to slice up vegetation.

0 m

The longest spines reached lengths of 30 cm (12 in).

Broad skull with protective horns.

Spine-covered tail protected the rear.

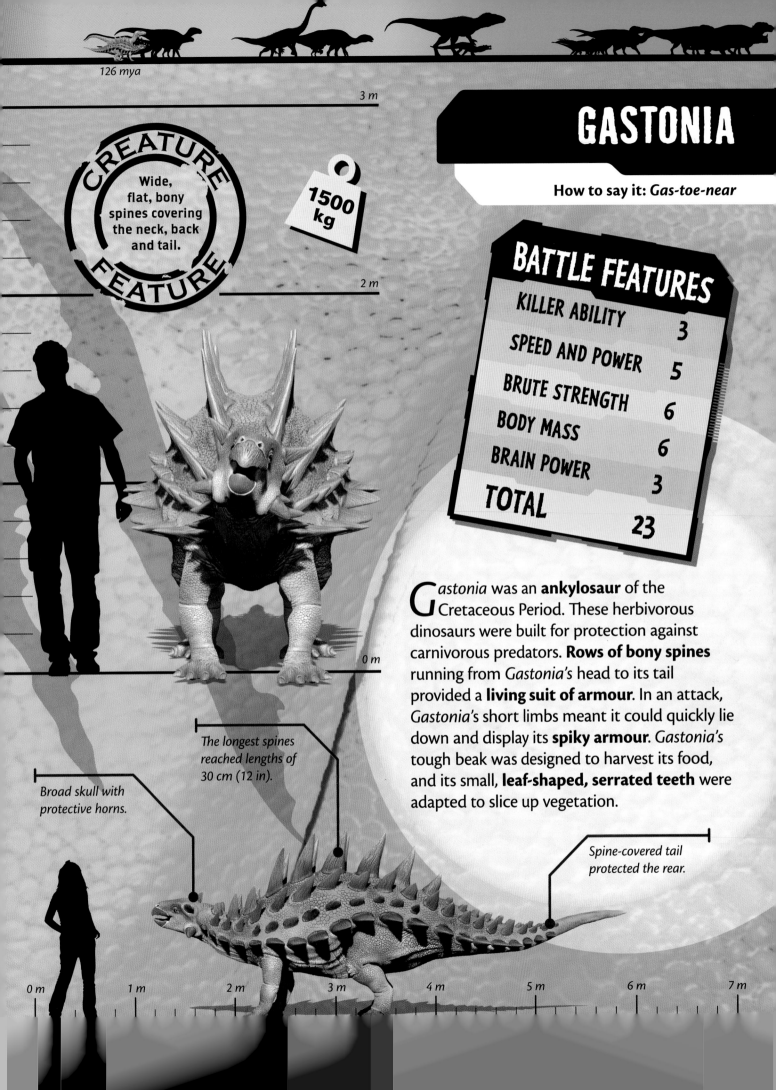

0 m   1 m   2 m   3 m   4 m   5 m   6 m   7 m

Surprise Attack

For once, top predator *Neovenator* has under estimated its prey. *Iguanodon* should have been an easy meal, but the herbivore is firmly defending its territory from its attacker. *Iguanodon*'s thumb-spike pushes deep into the chest of *Neovenator,* making it roar in pain. But can *Iguanodon* maintain the advantage? Can it really defeat a *Neovenator,* the dinosaur that is its natural predator?

IGUANODON

How to say it: Ig-gew-wah-no-don

BATTLE FEATURES

KILLER ABILITY	3
SPEED AND POWER	5
BRUTE STRENGTH	3
BODY MASS	3
BRAIN POWER	4
TOTAL	**18**

5000 kg

CREATURE FEATURE

Specialised hands with thumb-spike, three hooved fingers and thin, flexible fifth finger.

4 m

0 m

FOOTPRINTS IN TIME

As well as their bones, dinosaurs have left us some amazing fossilized tracks. This tyrannosaur footprint clearly shows its three toes – and also its huge size when compared with a human.

In 1825, *Iguanodon* became the second dinosaur to be named when its fossilized bones were found in Britain. Since then, *Iguanodon* fossils have been found in Asia, Europe and North America. Their **fossilized footprints** show that these herbivorous dinosaurs **moved around in herds**. Fully grown *Iguanodons* were almost certainly **quadrupeds** (walked on all fours) but younger animals might have been **bipeds**, walking on their hind limbs only.

Conical thumb-spike possibly used for defence.

Tail held horizontally off the ground.

Tendons in the back worked like a spring during running to increase speed.

Long, low skull comparable to a modern horse's

10 m   9 m   8 m   7 m   6 m   4 m   2 m   1 m   0 m

4 m

NEOVENATOR

How to say it: *Neo-ven-a-tor*

CREATURE FEATURE

A top predator of the Early Cretaceous.

2500 kg

2 m

1 m

0 m

BATTLE FEATURES

KILLER ABILITY	7
SPEED AND POWER	7
BRUTE STRENGTH	7
BODY MASS	5
BRAIN POWER	4
TOTAL	30

*N*eovenator, **new hunter**, was discovered on the Isle of Wight in Britain in 1978, but not named until 1996. It was a big, **predatory theropod**. *Neovenator* was light for its massive size, so it was probably an **agile animal**. This dangerous dinosaur would have preyed on plant-eaters such as *Iguanodon*. But many of *Neovenator's* fossil bones show signs of **healed injuries**, suggesting that it did not always escape unhurt.

Teeth so sharp they could cut into flesh like steak knives.

Toes tipped with pointed claws.

Claws on fingers could be 13 cm (5 in) long.

0 m | 1 m | 2 m | 3 m | 4 m | 6 m | 7 m | 8 m | 9 m | 10 m

The Earth Shakes

There is enough flesh on that sauropod to keep *Acrocanthosaurus* and its young alive for weeks. Only a bite to the neck will fell the vast titan, and this has to be delivered before *Sauroposeidon* can rear up on its hind legs and bring its vast weight crushing down on the predator. *Acrocanthosaurus* makes its move and breaks its cover. Four tonnes of predator push towards sixty tonnes of prey. The sauropod feels the sudden rush of movement, and instinctively lifts its front limbs while turning towards the blur of motion. The earth shakes as one giant predator and a mountain of prey square up to each other.

SAUROPOSEIDON

How to say it: *Saw-row-pos-side-don*

BATTLE FEATURES

KILLER ABILITY	3
SPEED AND POWER	8
BRUTE STRENGTH	9
BODY MASS	10
BRAIN POWER	4
TOTAL	**34**

When the **vast bones** of *Sauroposeidon* were first discovered, they were mistaken for fossilized tree trunks! Like all sauropods, *Sauroposeidon* had a large body, small head and a very long neck. Even the smallest sauropod was a **massive beast**, and the largest, *Argentinosaurus*, was an incredible 37 metres (120 feet) long. Experts are amazed that the sauropods became so enormous on a diet of just plants.

60 TONNES

15 m

10 m

5 m

0 m

CREATURE FEATURE

Sheer size – 16 m high, 34 m long – made this animal a top dinosaur.

FACT FLASH

Scientists don't know if *Sauroposeidon* actually stood up at its full height. It may have used its long neck to sweep the ground in a wide arc, collecting food.

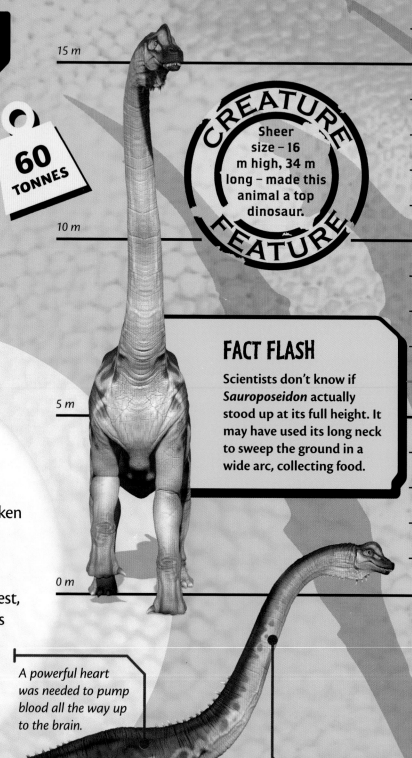

Ridged spikes may have run along back.

A powerful heart was needed to pump blood all the way up to the brain.

Neck was up to 12 m (39 ft), probably the longest of any sauropod's.

30 m　　25 m　　20 m　　　　　　　　　5 m　　0 m

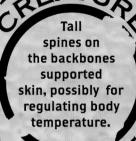

CREATURE

Tall spines on the backbones supported skin, possibly for regulating body temperature.

FEATURE

6000 kg

10 m

5 m

0 m

ACROCANTHOSAURUS

How to say it: *Acro-can-thow-saw-rus*

BATTLE FEATURES

KILLER ABILITY	8
SPEED AND POWER	8
BRUTE STRENGTH	8
BODY MASS	7
BRAIN POWER	6
TOTAL	37

Acrocanthosaurus was **one of the largest theropods** of the whole dinosaur age, and would have been the **top predator** in its environment. *Acrocanthosaurus* may have preyed on sauropods – especially the young, injured or elderly – and ornithopods. In North America, *Acrocanthosaurus* bones have been found alongside those of *Sauroposeidon*, showing that these **two giants** lived, or at least died, in the same area.

Skull was up to 1.2 m (4 ft) long – the height of an 8-year-old child.

Heavy tail counterblanced the head and body.

5 m   10 m   15 m   20 m   25 m   30 m

Cretaceous Kill

This gentle herbivore's food gathering trip is ending in a meal, but this time *Tenontosaurus* itself is on the menu. The luckless animal steadies itself on all fours as a pack of *Deinonychus* attacks. *Tenontosaurus* calls for members of its herd, but its voice is swallowed up by the dense forest. One of the predators grapples for a hold on the tough hide of its prey with its huge second toe-claw. Another circles to the front of the prey to deliver a bite to the throat. Will this flurry of teeth and claws signal the end for *Tenontosaurus*?

TENONTOSAURUS

How to say it: _Ten-nont-oh-saw-rus_

3 m

900 kg

BATTLE FEATURES

KILLER ABILITY	4
SPEED AND POWER	6
BRUTE STRENGTH	6
BODY MASS	7
BRAIN POWER	3
TOTAL	**26**

_T_enontosaurus belonged to a group of dinosaurs called the **Ornithopods**, herbivores that thrived in what is now North America in the Cretaceous Period. _Tenontosaurus_ may have stayed in **family groups**, possibly as defence against carnivorous attackers such as _Deinonychus_. A **gentle beast**, _Tenontosaurus_ would have spent much of its time chomping on tough plants.

Back crisscrossed by a network of bony tendons.

Horny beak for biting off tough plant parts.

7 m   6 m   5 m   4 m   1 m   0 m

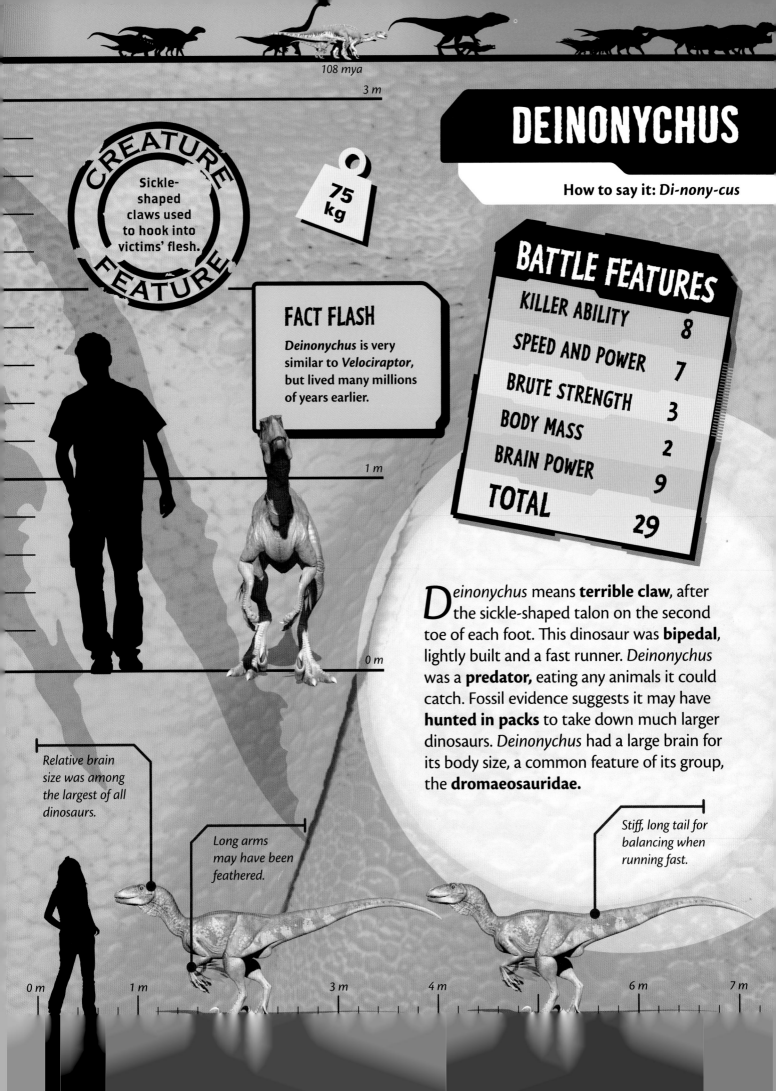

3 m

DEINONYCHUS

How to say it: *Di-nony-cus*

CREATURE FEATURE

Sickle-shaped claws used to hook into victims' flesh.

75 kg

FACT FLASH

Deinonychus is very similar to *Velociraptor*, but lived many millions of years earlier.

BATTLE FEATURES

KILLER ABILITY	8
SPEED AND POWER	7
BRUTE STRENGTH	3
BODY MASS	2
BRAIN POWER	9
TOTAL	29

1 m

0 m

*D*einonychus means **terrible claw**, after the sickle-shaped talon on the second toe of each foot. This dinosaur was **bipedal**, lightly built and a fast runner. *Deinonychus* was a **predator,** eating any animals it could catch. Fossil evidence suggests it may have **hunted in packs** to take down much larger dinosaurs. *Deinonychus* had a large brain for its body size, a common feature of its group, the **dromaeosauridae.**

Relative brain size was among the largest of all dinosaurs.

Long arms may have been feathered.

Stiff, long tail for balancing when running fast.

0 m   1 m   3 m   4 m   6 m   7 m

Crocodile Jaws

Spying a dozing *Carcharodontosaurus* on the shore, croc *Kaprosuchus* slithers out of the lake and spies the sleeping predator. Here is an opportunity it can't pass up. Using its stereoscopic vision, the croc lunges at the throat of the dozing giant. *Carcharodontosaurus* leaps awake, roaring with pain and alarm as dagger-like teeth tear into its flesh. It will need to fight hard for its life. The unforgiving jaws of *Kaprosuchus* could end the reign of this mighty predator.

KAPROSUCHUS

How to say it: *Cap-pro-sue-cus*

BATTLE FEATURES

KILLER ABILITY	8
SPEED AND POWER	7
BRUTE STRENGTH	4
BODY MASS	4
BRAIN POWER	4
TOTAL	**27**

CREATURE FEATURE

Tusk-like teeth in upper and lower jaws protruding from the mouth.

FACT FLASH

Kaprosuchus is only a little bigger than modern crocodiles, but the sturdy legs positioned right under its body would have allowed it to lunge out of the water and pursue prey on land.

900 kg

Kaprosuchus was a large **crocodylomorph** – a vast, semi-aquatic predator similar to a crocodile. Its name means **boar crocodile**, after its huge, pig-like, overlapping teeth. Just like today's crocodiles, *Kaprosuchus* would lie just beneath the water's surface at the edge of a river or lake, waiting for an unsuspecting victim to pass by. Then it would burst up, seize the terrified creature in its massive teeth and drag the prey to a **watery grave** – the perfect **ambush**!

Thick tail housed large muscles to propel body through water.

Small bony plates beneath the skin's surface provide excellent armour.

4 m

1 m

0 m

6 m

2 m

1 m

0 m

CARCHARODONTOSAURUS

How to say it: *Car-ca-ro-don-toe-saw-rus*

4 m

3 m

CREATURE FEATURE

Very powerful bite enhanced by blunt, broad skull.

BATTLE FEATURES

KILLER ABILITY	9
SPEED AND POWER	9
BRUTE STRENGTH	9
BODY MASS	9
BRAIN POWER	7
TOTAL	**43**

1 m

6000 kg

0 m

*C*archarodontosaurus lived in what is now North Africa, in the mid-Cretaceous Period. It was among the biggest and heaviest of the dinosaurs, and experts think it also had excellent eyesight. *Carcharadontosaurus* means **jagged tooth lizard** – this theropod's teeth were edged with **tiny, razor-sharp structures called denticles**, perfect for tearing into live flesh.

Heavy tail with powerful muscles to help locomotion.

Teeth up to 20 cm (8 in) long and well adapted to tear flesh.

Long and muscular legs for pursuing prey at up to 32 k/ph (20 mph).

0 m 1 m 2 m 3 m 4 m 6 m 8 m 9 m 10 m 11 m 12 m

Under Cover

A *Protoceratops* mother and her young concentrate on consuming another tough meal. So much chewing and grinding for so little nourishment. But they will soon have greater worries than finding their next meals, for their search for food has led them into *Velociraptor* territory. Even now, two of the predators are creeping towards the herbivores. They would not take on an adult *Protoceratops*, but the young are another matter. Without making a sound, the crafty carnivores slowly and deliberately move to an attack position...

The Fight Back

Seeing a flash of claws and teeth, the *Protoceratops* react fast – and run for their lives. The chase begins, but inevitably the young can't keep up with its mother. The infant herbivore is snapped up and carried off. The mother turns to give chase, and finds itself face-to-face with another predator. With a bellow of fury, the *Protoceratops* launches an attack, biting down hard on the *Velociraptor's* arm. The aggressor responds by frantically stabbing at the *Protoceratops's* belly with its sickle-shaped claw. Can the herbivore manoeuvre its superior body weight to crush its foe? Or will the *Velociraptor* come out on top?

VELOCIRAPTOR

How to say it: *Vel-oh-sir-rap-tor*

BATTLE FEATURES

KILLER ABILITY	8
SPEED AND POWER	6
BRUTE STRENGTH	2
BODY MASS	2
BRAIN POWER	8
TOTAL	**26**

CREATURE FEATURE

Specialized climbing claw on second toe of each foot.

1 m

25 kg

EYE-SPY

This model of a skull of *Velociraptor* shows eye sockets known as orbits. Keen eyesight would have been an important hunting ability. *Velociraptor*'s unusually large orbits suggest that it may have been able to hunt in the semi-darkness of twilight.

There is strong evidence that this small dinosaur was an active predator and even a **pack-hunter.** It was relatively smart for a dinosaur and could have used this intelligence to communicate with the pack. The long, narrow skull was packed with backward-curved, sharply serrated teeth. The second toe of each foot sported a **massive claw.** Experts believe that *Velocipraptor* used this as a hook to help climb onto and hold its prey.

Long, thin tail braced by bony projections, but slightly flexible.

Second toe-claw raised off the ground.

Narrow fingers ending in sharp claws.

1.5 m   1 m   0.5 m   0 m

1 m

PROTOCERATOPS

How to say it: *Pro-toe-sera-tops*

190 kg

Large frill, made of bone and skin, at the back of the skull.

0.5 m

BATTLE FEATURES

KILLER ABILITY	3
SPEED AND POWER	3
BRUTE STRENGTH	4
BODY MASS	5
BRAIN POWER	1
TOTAL	**16**

This small, horned dinosaur is one of the **first Ceratopsians**, a group that would eventually lead to *Triceratops*. *Protoceratop's* **deep skull** and massive lower jaws look fierce, but were adapted to cut through the tough vegetation that made up this herbivore's diet. There is strong evidence that *Protoceratops* lived in **large groups,** especially when **nesting**. This is no surprise, given that it shared an environment with the fierce *Velociraptor!*

Enlarged bones at the back of the skull form the frill.

Parrot-like beak.

Long legs suggests Protoceratops *was a fast runner.*

0 m   0.5 m   1 m   1.5 m   2 m

Wounding Teeth

It is the Late Cretaceous Period and horn-faced dinosaurs dominate the forests of North America. They may be numerous, but they are no match for one particularly intelligent predatory dinosaur, *Troodon*. Just a fraction of the weight of this *Avaceratops*, *Troodon* is nonetheless capable of torturing the horn-face into submission. It darts forwards to peck at the animal's hide again and again, its razor-sharp serrated teeth tearing jagged holes in the *Avaceratop's* flesh. Away from the safety of its herd, the herbivore is paralyzed by fear of this relentless attacker.

TROODON

How to say it: *True-oh-don*

FACT FLASH

Troodon was the most northerly known dinosaur. Its remains were found in a part of Russia that would have been only 1,000km from the North Pole during the time *Troodon* was alive.

BATTLE FEATURES

KILLER ABILITY	8
SPEED AND POWER	6
BRUTE STRENGTH	2
BODY MASS	2
BRAIN POWER	10
TOTAL	**28**

CREATURE FEATURE

A line of very large serrations runs along the front and back edges of teeth.

0.5 m

50 kg

0 m

*T*roodon was one of the **smartest dinosaurs**, with a very large brain for its body size. Its name means **wounding tooth**, after its razor-sharp, saw-edged teeth. Even fossilized ones can be dangerous and palaeontologists have to take extra care when handling them. *Troodon*'s large eyes enabled it to see potential prey in dim light, before the prey spotted it, in the shadows of the Cretaceous forests.

Jaw packed with almost 100 teeth.

Troodon swung its lower legs as it walked, much like a modern bird.

4 m   3 m   2 m   0 m

2 m

900 kg

Large cutting area on the beak, formed partly by the 'rostral bone'.

AVACERATOPS

How to say it: Ava-sera-tops

BATTLE FEATURES

KILLER ABILITY	2
SPEED AND POWER	4
BRUTE STRENGTH	6
BODY MASS	8
BRAIN POWER	2
TOTAL	**22**

1 m

0.5 m

0 m

Many **ceratopsian dinosaurs** were discovered over 100 years ago by the first palaeontologists, but this species was not found until 1986. Like all ceratopsian dinosaurs, *Avaceratops* was a herbivore and had a **powerful beak** that would cut through foliage. The first ceratopsians were only about one metre long, but later ones, such as *Avaceratops*, were as big as bulls.

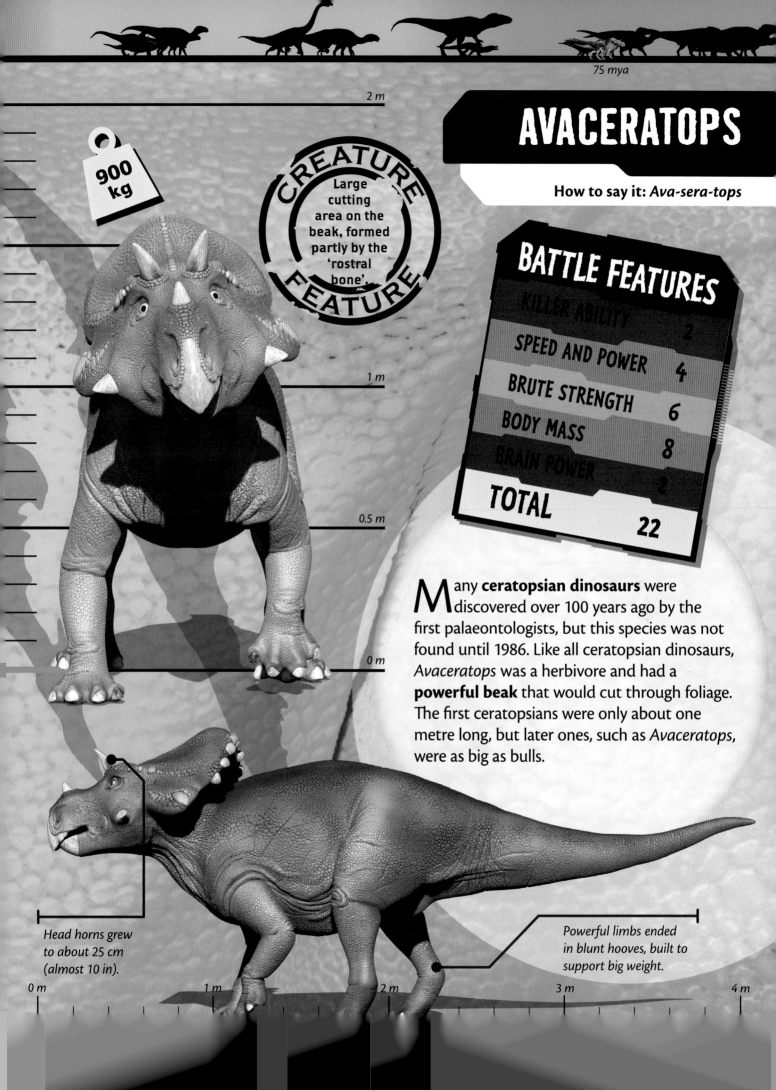

Head horns grew to about 25 cm (almost 10 in).

Powerful limbs ended in blunt hooves, built to support big weight.

0 m   1 m   2 m   3 m   4 m

The Last Lunge

One of the *Parasaurolophus* herd has been injured and the other members can hear it bellowing in pain. Like all hadrosaurs, the *Parasaurolophus* can make deep, booming sounds through its head crest. The herd rushes towards the stricken sound, but an adult *Gorgosaurus* has responded to the call too. The *Gorgosaurus* stumbles clumsily into their path, its right leg dragging on the ground. It seems to be injured. Nevertheless the *Gorgosaurus* lunges at the closest *Parasaurolophus*. It is aiming for a crushing bite that will break the animal's spine, but its jaws are too weak to make contact with the bone. Can the hadrosaurs shake off this annoying predator and continue their rescue operation?

GORGOSAURUS

How to say it: *Gore-go-saw-rus*

4 m

2500 kg

MONSTER CALLS

What kind of noises did dinosaurs make? Large meat-eaters like *T. rex* almost certainly made sounds to communicate, while the crested dinosaurs might have called to one another by inhaling air through hollow chambers in their head crests. We might never know how giant bodied, small headed herbivores like *Diplodocus* may have sounded.

BATTLE FEATURES

KILLER ABILITY	8
SPEED AND POWER	9
BRUTE STRENGTH	10
BODY MASS	9
BRAIN POWER	8
TOTAL	**44**

CREATURE FEATURE

Awesomely powerful jaws, capable of a bone-crushing bite.

Gorgosaurus was a member of the biggest and fiercest dinosaur group – the **tyrannosaurs**. Like other tyrannosaurs, *Gorgosaurus* was a **top predator**, a massive beast with huge legs, short arms and immensely powerful jaws. *Gorgosaurus* would have preyed on the many plant-eating dinosaurs that shared its environment, perhaps picking off weak members of the herd.

*Enlarged bone above the eye formed a **distinctive crest**.*

Like a bird, Gorgosaurus walked on three toes.

Tiny arms end in three-fingered hands.

10 m 9 m 8 m 7 m 6 m 5 m 4 m 3 m 2 m 1 m 0 m

2500 kg

PARASAUROLOPHUS

How to say it: *Para-low-four-saw-rus*

CREATURE
A skull like a big, bony banana!
FEATURE

2 m

1 m

0 m

BATTLE FEATURES

KILLER ABILITY	4
SPEED AND POWER	7
BRUTE STRENGTH	7
BODY MASS	8
BRAIN POWER	3
TOTAL	**29**

This curious looking beast was a **lambeosaur** – a duck-billed, crested dinosaur. The crest contained **a series of tubes connecting the nose to the throat**. Lambeosaurs probably used their crests to make **sounds**, perhaps to call to one another. The bones of *Parasaurolophus* have been found with healed bite marks from predatory dinosaurs, showing that it sometimes escaped its attackers.

Distinctive head crest.

Rare fossils indicate the fingers were joined by a mitten-like covering of skin.

Parasaurolophus was both bipedal and quadrupedal.

0 m   1 m   2 m   3 m   5 m   6 m   7 m   8 m   9 m   10 m

A Chance Ambush

The day is warm and still and the sun high in the sky. A group of *Albertosaurus* is dozing in the cool shade of some monkey puzzle trees when a family of *Hypacrosaurus* ambles into their view. The herbivores begin grazing in the clearing, unaware of the three predators nearby. Suddenly alert, the *Albertosaurus* rise stealthily to their feet. Two prowl around the fearful *Hypacrosaurus* family. The roar of these two attackers distracts the prey from the silent, large male beast on their right side. It is selecting which animal to isolate for an attack.

The young *Hypacrosaurus* makes a desperate lunge away from its assailant – only to find itself head-to-head with another pack member. Instantly, the powerful jaws of *Albertosaurus* clamp down hard on the base of the prey's neck. The sound of bones breaking brings a triumphant roar from the hungry pack. Dinner is served.

ALBERTOSAURUS

How to say it: *Alber-toe-saw-rus*

BATTLE FEATURES

KILLER ABILITY	7
SPEED AND POWER	7
BRUTE STRENGTH	7
BODY MASS	6
BRAIN POWER	6
TOTAL	**33**

This **tyrannosaur** gets its name from the province of Alberta in Canada, where the bones of more than 30 animals have been discovered. The forested landscape, crisscrossed by rivers, would have been a **rich hunting ground** for this predatory dinosaur. Fossil evidence points to *Albertosaurus* being a **pack-hunter** – a scary prospect for its potential prey.

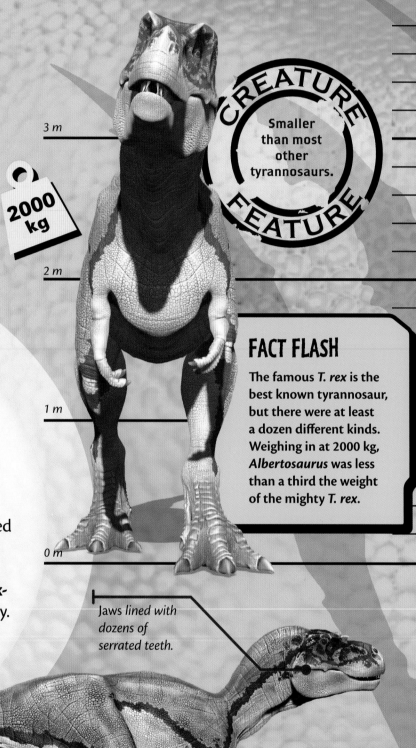

4 m

3 m

2 m

1 m

0 m

2000 kg

CREATURE FEATURE

Smaller than most other tyrannosaurs.

FACT FLASH

The famous *T. rex* is the best known tyrannosaur, but there were at least a dozen different kinds. Weighing in at 2000 kg, *Albertosaurus* was less than a third the weight of the mighty *T. rex*.

Jaws *lined with dozens of serrated teeth.*

Short arms ending in two fingers, like other tyrannosaurs.

Bones of Albertosaurus suggest it reached adult size at 15–20 years-old.

10 m 9 m 8 m 7 m 6 m 4 m 3 m 2 m 1 m 0 m

4 m

3 m

CREATURE FEATURE

Tall backbones unlike other lambeosaurs.

4000 kg

3 m

2 m

1 m

0 m

HYPACROSAURUS

How to say it: *High-pack-row-saw-rus*

BATTLE FEATURES

KILLER ABILITY	3
SPEED AND POWER	6
BRUTE STRENGTH	8
BODY MASS	8
BRAIN POWER	3
TOTAL	**28**

Hypacrosaurus was one of the biggest dinosaurs of its time. Like other lambeosaurs, it was a bipedal and quadrupedal herbivore, and had a **head crest and a duck bill**. From studying fossilized tracks, experts think that lambeosaurs probably **lived in herds.** There is also evidence that they may have formed **nesting colonies**, just as some birds do.

Backbone has bony neural spines.

Relatively *delicate* forelimbs indicate that most weight was borne by the hind legs.

Tail was once though to be used for swimming, but experts now know Hypacrosaurus *lived on land.*

0 m   1 m   2 m   3 m   6 m   7 m   8 m   9 m   10 m

Desert Encounter

We are in what is now Mongolia's Gobi Desert, where Cretacaeous dinosaurs are plentiful. This *Tarbosaurus* has approached the heavily armoured *Tarchia* out of curiosity – edging closer to inspect and sniff it. The *Tarchia* becomes irritated with the attention and swiftly turns away, deliberately swinging its heavy tail club at the body of the other animal. Taken by surprise, the predator lifts its right leg to avoid the club and finds itself unbalanced on its left foot. Angry now, the predator lets out a roar, but will it dare to take revenge on the impenetrable creature, or will it just slope off?

TARBOSAURUS

How to say it: *Tar-bow-saw-rus*

6000 kg

BATTLE FEATURES

KILLER ABILITY	9
SPEED AND POWER	8
BRUTE STRENGTH	8
BODY MASS	9
BRAIN POWER	8
TOTAL	**42**

This huge predator from what is now Mongolia would have lived up to its name, **alarming lizard.** Like most other tyrannosaurs, *Tarbosaurus* was a dangerous predator – it was at the top of the food chain. Its skull was uniquely adapted for making an extra-hard, **bone-crushing bite**. This could have enabled *Tarbosaurus* to attack prey much larger than itself, maybe even massive sauropods.

WHAT'S IN AN NAME?

'Alarming lizard' is a pretty good name for something that looks like *Tarbosaurus*. Some dinosaurs are named for how they look (*Triceratops* means 'three-horned-face'), some are named for where they were found (*Utahraptor* was found in Utah), and some are named after the people who discovered them (*Herrerasaurus* was discovered by Victorino Herrera). In fact, dinosaur itself just means 'terrible lizard'.

CREATURE FEATURE

Lower jaw adapted to deliver a super-powerful bite.

Skull perfectly adapted to deliver bone-crushing bites.

Large hip-bones provided stability for big leg muscles.

Short arms, even for a tyrannosaur.

12 m   11 m   10 m   9 m   8 m   7 m   5 m   4 m   3 m   2 m   1 m   0 m

5 m

4 m

How to say it: *Tah-che-a*

CREATURE FEATURE

Biggest ankylosaur (armoured dinosaur).

4500 kg

3 m

2 m

BATTLE FEATURES

KILLER ABILITY	2
SPEED AND POWER	6
BRUTE STRENGTH	8
BODY MASS	9
BRAIN POWER	2
TOTAL	27

Covered in bony spines, *Tarchia* was an **armour-plated tank** of a dinosaur. Rows of spikes along its body provided top protection from predators' jaws. Several of the backbones at the end of its tail were enlarged and adapted into a **thick, bony club**. It would take a very persistent attacker to fight its way past such **effective defences**!

Sturdy limbs ending in hoof-like claws.

Horny beak with jaws that housed delicate, leaf-shaped teeth.

Tail club could smash predators' leg bones.

0 m   1 m   2 m   3 m   5 m   7 m   8 m   9 m   10 m   11 m   12 m

Killing Blow

These titans twist and turn around one another, each trying to deliver the killing blow. *T. rex* is the mightiest predator to have walked the Earth. Its rival is a *Triceratops* – a hulking giant built for both defence and offence. Both animals are fighting fit, but only one will walk away from this battle. *Triceratops* raises its mighty horns, while pushing its vast bulk towards the ground, presenting its array of horns to *T. rex*. Soon, the tough horns drip with the blood of the attacker. But *T. rex* out-manoeuvres its opponent to get behind *Triceratop*'s head-frill, clamping its colossal jaws around the softer neck hide.

TYRANNOSAURUS REX

How to say it: *Tie-ran-oh-saw-rus-rex*

BATTLE FEATURES

KILLER ABILITY	10
SPEED AND POWER	10
BRUTE STRENGTH	9
BODY MASS	8
BRAIN POWER	9
TOTAL	46

The **tyrant lizard king** is the biggest land predator ever and the world's most famous dinosaur. *T. rex* was as **big as an African elephant**, could run as fast as an **Olympic sprinter**, had **super senses** for hearing, smell and sight and had **teeth as long and sharp as carving knives**. *T. rex* had a lot of hunting to do – this massive predator would have needed to eat the weight of two human beings every day just to keep going!

7000 kg

2 m

1 m

CREATURE FEATURE

Biggest and strongest jaws of any dinosaur.

TINY T.REX?

The *T. rex* was certainly mighty, but it had surprisingly weedy arms. The most important parts of its body were its powerful legs and huge jaws. Its arms may simply not have been used very much.

Bite force equivalent to dropping the weight of a car onto your toe!

Massive jaws up to 1.2 metres (4 ft) long.

Powerful legs enabled T. rex to run at speeds of up to 20 mph (32 k/ph).

Each arm could lift up to 400 kg (880 lb).

12 m   11 m   10 m   9 m   8 m   7 m   4 m   3 m   2 m   1 m   0 m

4 m

1200 kg

TRICERATOPS

How to say it: *Tri-sera-tops*

CREATURE FEATURE

Triceratops means three-horned-face.

BATTLE FEATURES

KILLER ABILITY	2
SPEED AND POWER	4
BRUTE STRENGTH	8
BODY MASS	10
BRAIN POWER	4
TOTAL	28

This Late Cretaceous herbivore lived alongside some big predators, including the mighty *T. rex*. The huge frill around the head was a **solid sheet of bone crisscrossed by blood vessels**. It anchored the huge jaw muscles and might also have helped **regulate body temperature**, like the bony plates of *Stegosaurus*. The huge belly provided room for a **vast stomach** to extract the nutrients from its diet of tough plants.

Rear end was sometimes the target site for T. rex bites, shown by many fossils.

Horn covering was a tough, keratin-like material, similar to human fingernails.

Chunky tail housed large muscles.

0 m 1 m 2 m 3 m 4 m 8 m 9 m 10 m 11 m 12 m

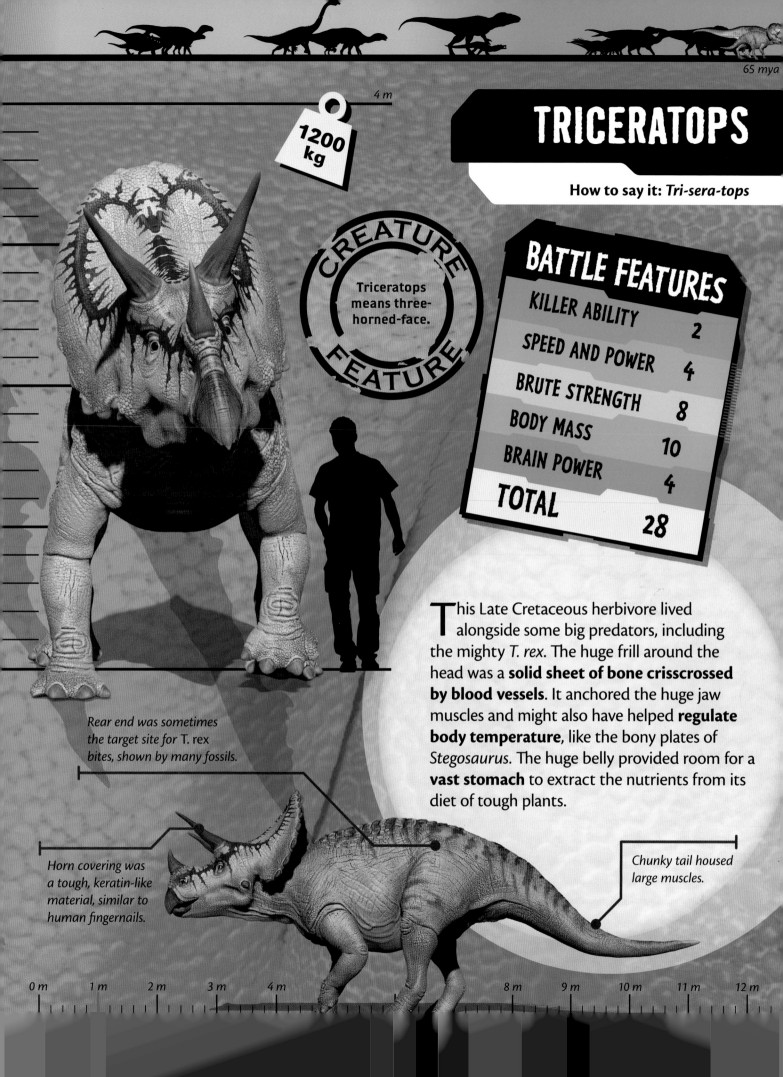

THE RESULTS!

Which of these titans won the war? Who was meat, who lived to fight another day, and who was a true victor?

Jaws

Herrerasaurus vs Eoraptor p6

Eoraptor didn't have the strength and mass of its predator, but it was fast enough to escape *Herrerasaurus*.

Fresh Meat

Dilophosaurus vs Anchisaurus p10

The slowest of those *Anchisaurus* was felled by the crested beast. Fresh meat for *Dilophosaurus*!

Cornered

Megalosaurus vs Camptosaurus p14

The superior strength and speed of *Megalosaurus* won over and it was toast for *Camptosaurus*.

Predator Trap

Allosaurus vs Stegosaurus p18

After a long battle, *Stegosaurus's* crushed skull proved fatal. A wounded *Allosaurus* was the victor.

Clashing Cousins

Archaeopteryx vs Compsognathus p22

Of these two weeds, *Compsognathus* was the stronger animal, but *Archaeopteryx* could simply fly away!

Claws on Armour

Utahraptor vs Gastonia p26

Utahraptor used its superior battle skills to pierce *Gastonia's* spiky defence to overcome the hapless herbivore.

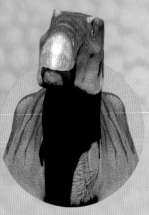

Surprise Attack

Iguanodon vs Neovenator p30

For once, *Neovenator* loped off licking its wounds! *Iguanodon* was the unlikely victor of this battle.

The Earth Shakes

Sauroposeidon vs Acrocanthosaurus p36

Even 60 tonnes of sauropod could not stand up to top predator *Acrocanthosaurus*.

Cretaceous Kill

Tenontosaurus vs Deinonychus p38

Wandering away from the herd was a big mistake. Poor *Tenontosaurus* didn't stand a chance against a pack of fierce *Deinonychus*

Crocodile Jaws

Carcharadontosaurus vs Kaprosuchus p42

Carcharadontosaurus was too heavy to drag into the water to drown, so *Kaprosuchus* had to abandon its prey. No winner – or loser – in this battle.

The Fight Back

Velociraptor vs Protoceratops p48

Two losers! Both the battling dinosaurs died in a fatal embrace.

Wounding Teeth

Troodon vs Avaceratops p52

Troodon succeeded in severely wounding the terrified *Avaceratops*. Then it left the herbivore to become easy prey for bigger carnivores.

The Last Lunge

Gorgosaurus vs Parasaurolophus p56

That old *Gorgosaurus* was on its last legs. The herd easily fought it off and continued with their mission.

In For The Kill

Albertosaurus vs Hypacrosaurus p62

No question of the outcome here! *Hypacrosaurus* was quickly turned into a fine feast for the carnivores.

Desert Encounter

Tarbosaurus vs Tarchia p66

A surprise result for low-scoring *Tarchia*. The armoured dino scared the tyrannosaur into making a retreat.

Killing Blow

T. rex vs Triceratops p70

Triceratops put up a brave fight, but did he ever really stand a chance? No dinosaur, not even three-horned-face, gets to lick the T!

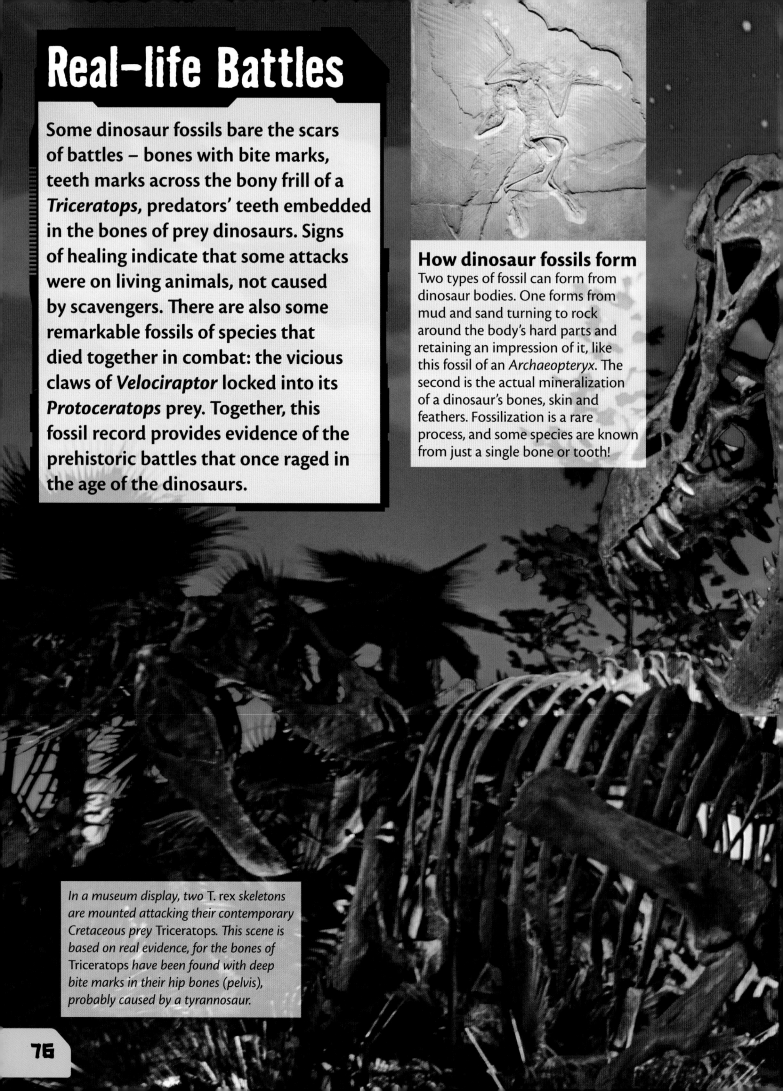

Real-life Battles

Some dinosaur fossils bare the scars of battles – bones with bite marks, teeth marks across the bony frill of a *Triceratops*, predators' teeth embedded in the bones of prey dinosaurs. Signs of healing indicate that some attacks were on living animals, not caused by scavengers. There are also some remarkable fossils of species that died together in combat: the vicious claws of *Velociraptor* locked into its *Protoceratops* prey. Together, this fossil record provides evidence of the prehistoric battles that once raged in the age of the dinosaurs.

How dinosaur fossils form

Two types of fossil can form from dinosaur bodies. One forms from mud and sand turning to rock around the body's hard parts and retaining an impression of it, like this fossil of an *Archaeopteryx*. The second is the actual mineralization of a dinosaur's bones, skin and feathers. Fossilization is a rare process, and some species are known from just a single bone or tooth!

In a museum display, two T. rex skeletons are mounted attacking their contemporary Cretaceous prey Triceratops. This scene is based on real evidence, for the bones of Triceratops have been found with deep bite marks in their hip bones (pelvis), probably caused by a tyrannosaur.

In Montana, USA, a dinosaur dig team excavates the remains of one of the mightiest predators, Tyrannosaurus rex. Among a dig team are a photographer and artist, to make a detailed record of the site, in case it provides clues about the dinosaur's life. The bones, such as this lower leg, will be taken to a laboratory for specialist cleaning.

Glossary

Ankylosaur

A group of armour-plated herbivorous dinosaurs that appeared in the Jurassic and persisted till the end of the Cretaceous Periods.

Biped

An animal that walks on its hind-legs and does not use its arms in locomotion.

Carnivore

An animal that eats mostly meat – dead or alive.

Ceratopsians

A group of dinosaurs that includes *Triceratops* and all its horned and beak-faced relations.

Cretaceous Period

Lasted from 145–66 million years ago and represent the last period of time in which dinosaurs dominated the Earth.

Denticles

Small bony plates that can form within or the surface of an animals skin.

Dromaeosauridae

A distinct family of bird-like predatory dinosaurs that became common in the Late Cretaceous.

Duckbill

A nickname for hadrosaur dinosaurs after their broad mouth that resembled the bill of a very large duck!

Extinct

The global and total loss of multiple or single species.

Food chain

The relationship of what is eaten and the links between species in a distinct environment.

Fossil

The preserved remains (such as bones and teeth) or traces (such as tracks) of life on Earth.

Fossil record

All the known fossils through geological time.

Fossil specimen

A single fossil that might be studied by a palaeontologist.

Herbivore

An animal that only eats plants in its diet.

Hunting ground

An area where an animal hunts its prey.

Jurassic Period

Lasted from 201–145 million years ago and marks the time (175 million years ago) when the supercontinent Pangaea started to break-up.

Lambeosaurs

A group of late Cretaceous herbivorous hadrosaur dinosaurs that often sported crests upon their heads.

Mesozoic Era

The time between 251–66 mya, which scientists divide into three periods, the Triassic, Jurassic and Cretaceous. The Mesozoic Era is sometimes called The Age of the Dinosaurs.

Nesting

An animal that builds a structure in which to raise its young. Birds build nests from twigs and leaves and dinosaurs kicked earth into a mound.

Ornithischian

Means 'bird-hipped' and is applied to all dinosaurs that had a distinct bone structure to their hips, which looked like a birds' hips, but these dinosaurs did not give rise to birds!

Ornithopods
A hugely successful group of herbivorous ornithischian dinosaurs.

Pack-hunter
A predator that actively works with members of its own species to hunt and attack prey.

Palaeontologist
A scientist who studies the traces and fossil remains of extinct plants and animals..

Pangaea
One massive continent that covered the Earth from 300 million years ago until its break up around 175 million years ago.

Predator
An animal that actively hunts, captures and eats other animals.

Prey
An animal that is hunted and eaten by predators.

Quadruped
An animal that walks using both its arms and legs, literally on all fours.

Reptile
A group of animals that became adapted to lay eggs on land and survive in harsher conditions than their water-based ancestors.

Saurischian
Means 'lizard-hipped' and refers to a group that includes the sauropod and theropod dinosaurs.

Sauropod
Saurishian herbivores with long necks, small heads, long tails and large quadrupedal bodies.

Species
A distinct group of plants or animals that can reproduce to create offspring.

Stegosaurs
A group of dinosaurs with rows of bony plates or spines running down their backs.

Territory
A discrete area within an environment where an animal claims to live and often defends from competing members of its own and other species.

Theropod
This name literally means 'beast-foot' and is applied to all predatory dinosaurs and their descendants, the birds!.

Triassic Period
Lasted from 252–201 million years ago and marks the first appearance of dinosaurs.

Tyrannosaur
A term used to group together close relatives of Tyrannosaurus, such as *Tarbosaurus*.

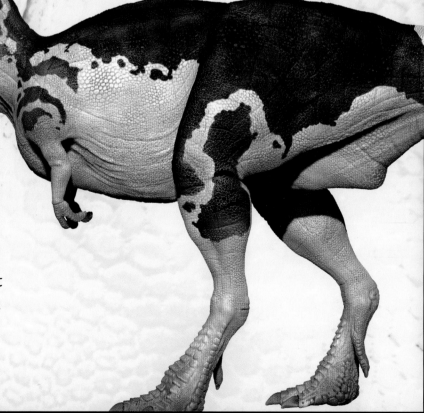

Index

A

Acrocanthosaurus 34, 37, 74
Albertosaurus 60, 62, 64, 75
Allosaurus 18, 20, 74
Anchisaurus 11, 13, 74
ankylosaurs 29, 69
Archaeopteryx 23, 24, 74, 76
Argentinosaurus 36
armoured dinosaurs 5, 21, 26, 29, 44, 69
Avaceratops 53, 55, 75

B

beaks 17, 29, 40, 51, 55, 69
bipedal dinosaurs 17, 25, 28, 32, 41, 59, 65
'bird-feet' dinosaurs see ornithopods
birds 5, 23, 24
body temperature 21, 37, 73
bony plates and projections 21, 44, 50
brains 21, 41, 54, 68

C

calls and other noises 58, 59
Camptosaurus 14, 17, 74
Carcharodontosaurus 42, 45, 75
carnivores 5, 6, 9, 11, 12, 16
ceratopsians 5, 51, 55
claws 20, 24, 26, 28, 33, 39, 41, 50, 69
club tails 67, 69
Compsognathus 23, 25, 74
crests 12, 56, 58, 59, 65
Cretaceous Period 4, 28, 29, 40, 45, 53, 67, 73
crocodylomorphs 44

DE

death of the dinosaurs 5
Deinonychus 39, 41, 75
denticles 45
Dilophosaurus 11, 12, 74
Diplodocus 58
dromaeosaurids 20, 28, 41
duck bills 59, 65
Eoraptor 6, 9, 74
extinction 5, 9
eyesight 45, 50, 54, 68

F

feathered dinosaurs 24, 25, 41
flying dinosaurs 23, 24
food chain 68
footprints, fossilized 32
fossilization process 76
fossils 4, 12, 16, 17, 24, 32, 54, 64, 76–7
frills 51, 71, 73

G

Gastonia 26, 29, 74
geological time periods 4
Gorgosaurus 56, 58, 75

H

hadrosaurs 5, 56
hands 9, 16, 17, 20, 32, 58
herbivores 5, 11, 13, 17, 18, 21, 29, 30, 32, 36, 39, 40, 46, 51, 53, 55, 60, 65, 73
herds 32, 51, 56, 65
Herrerasaurus 6, 8, 68, 74
hooves 55
horns 4, 5, 29, 53, 55, 71, 73
Hypacrosaurus 60, 62, 65, 75

IJK

Iguanodon 30, 32, 74
intelligence 28, 41, 50, 54
Jaws 20, 24, 58, 68, 72
Jurassic Period 4, 11, 12, 20, 23
Kaprosuchus 42, 44, 75

LM

lambeosaurs 59, 65
Megalosaurus 14, 16, 74
Mesozoic Era 4

N

names of dinosaurs 68
necks 13, 36
Neovenator 30, 33, 74
nesting 51, 65
northerly dinosaurs 54

O

orbits (eye sockets) 9, 50
ornithischians 5
ornithopods 17, 37, 40

P

pack-hunters 41, 50, 64
palaeontologists 54, 55
Pangaea 4
Parasaurolophus 56, 59, 75
predatory dinosaurs 8, 9, 14, 18, 20, 28, 30, 33, 37, 39, 41, 50, 53, 58, 64, 67, 68, 72
Protoceratops 46, 49, 51, 75, 76

QR

quadrupedal dinosaurs 13, 17, 32, 59, 65
running speeds 12, 45, 72

S

saurischians 5
sauropods 5, 13, 34, 36, 37, 68
Sauroposeidon 34, 36, 37, 74
semi-aquatic dinosaurs 44
skulls 9, 21, 29, 32, 37, 50, 51, 59, 68
smell, sense of 12
spikes and spines 21, 26, 29, 30, 32, 36, 37, 65, 69
Stegosaurus 18, 21, 74

T

tails 13, 17, 24, 25, 28, 29, 32, 37, 40, 41, 44, 45, 50, 67, 69
Tarbosaurus 67, 68, 75
Tarchia 67, 69, 75
teeth 8, 9, 16, 17, 28, 29, 33, 44, 45, 50, 54, 64, 69, 72
Tenontosaurus 39, 40, 75
theropods 5, 16, 20, 24, 33, 37, 45
top predators 28, 33, 37, 58, 68
Triassic Period 4, 6
Triceratops 51, 68, 71, 73, 75, 76
Troodon 53, 54, 75
tyrannosaurs 4, 5, 58, 64, 68
Tyrannosaurus rex 8, 58, 64, 71, 72, 75, 76, 77

UVW

Utahraptor 26, 28, 68, 74
Velociraptor 41, 46, 49, 50, 75, 76